HOW TO BEAT THE IRS

INSIDER TACTICS

Ms. X

BOARDROOM® BOOKS

330 West 42nd Street, New York, New York 10036

Library of Congress Cataloging in Publication Data

Ms. X.
  How to beat the IRS.

  1. Tax administration and procedure—United States.
2. Tax auditing—United States. 3. Tax protests and
appeals—United States. 4. United States. Internal
Revenue Service. I. Title. II. Title: How to beat the
I.R.S.
KF6300.Z9M7 1983   343.7305'23   83-21549
ISBN 0-932648-49-5   347.303523

Printed in the United States of America

Contents

Chapter 9

Chapter 10

Chapter 11

Appendix / 65

Introduction

I thought of calling this book <u>The Answers to Most of the Questions People Have Asked Me About How to Get Out of (or Avoid) Trouble with the IRS</u>.

I chose <u>How to Beat the IRS</u> because it's easier to remember and more intriguing.

The title is a bit ironic, because the key to success with the IRS is to do very little actual fighting but to be <u>armed</u> with the right information. You have to know what the IRS can and cannot do and how it's likely to react in any given situation. By penetrating the mystique surrounding the IRS, you may neutralize the tremendous advantage it has whenever it chooses to focus its resources on one person. When you are informed, the "fight" is fairer and the odds of your emerging a winner are considerably improved.

<u>How to Beat the IRS</u> is packed with important and interesting information you need to know. It will help you understand the IRS, its procedures, its strengths and weaknesses. And it is a source book of ideas. But it is not a replacement for the skilled tax practitioner you should have at your side when you do battle with the IRS. To modify an old courthouse saying: A person who acts as his own tax advisor has a fool for a client.

<u>How to Beat the IRS</u> will give you the essential background you need and a general understanding of what happens when you become involved with the IRS. And it will give you the knowledge and insight you will need to select a good accountant or lawyer to help you--one who really knows how the IRS works. What's

more, after reading this special report you will be able to communicate clearly with your representative and to effectively assist him in planning a strategy to fight the IRS and <u>win</u>.

Ms. X

Chapter 1
Keeping a Low
Audit Profile

One of the questions most often asked of accountants and tax attorneys by their clients is "Will I be audited if I deduct this item?" Unfortunately, not even the most brilliant tax practitioner can give 100 percent assurance that a client will not be audited if a particular deduction is taken. The exact criteria used by the IRS computers to determine which returns will be audited is a closely guarded secret, but knowledgeable people in the profession develop a sixth sense as to what is likely to trigger further IRS scrutiny.

What Is Your Audit Risk?

Contrary to what most people believe, most tax returns are not audited. The IRS is incapable of examining all the returns it should simply because of shortages of people, money, and time. The time problem is caused by the statute of limitations, which generally requires that the IRS assess any additional tax within three years from the date a tax return is filed. Since the statute of limitations is constantly running, the IRS has its own rules about when it will initiate a tax audit. If a return has not been selected for audit within 24 months of the date it has been filed, it takes exceptional reasons to begin an audit after that.

The latest IRS public statistics reveal that only 1.31 percent of all individual tax returns filed are audited. The percentage is actually a bit higher since many of the returns included in the 1.31 percent figure are 1040-A short forms, which are usually not examined. Even if the returns that would probably

not be audited were eliminated from consideration, the percentage of audited returns would increase only to the 3 to 4 percent level. What this means is that your chances of being audited are slim.

The IRS district you live in may affect the odds of being audited. In the Manhattan district, for example, 1.9 percent of all individual tax returns filed are audited, whereas in Dallas, the rate is only 1.2 percent. Figure 1-1 shows the percentage of individual returns audited in various IRS districts. It will give you an idea of which areas are the most audit prone in the country.

IRS District	Percent of Individual Returns Audited
Anchorage	2.4
Atlanta	1.0
Baltimore	1.1
Boston	0.7
Brooklyn	1.2
Chicago	0.8
Cleveland	0.9
Dallas	1.2
Detroit	0.9
Greensboro	0.9
Indianapolis	0.6
Jacksonville	1.1
Los Angeles	1.7
Manhattan	1.9
Milwaukee	0.7
Newark	1.0
Philadelphia	0.7
Pittsburgh	0.7
Richmond	0.9
San Francisco	2.0
St. Louis	0.9

1-1. Percentages of returns audited for selected IRS districts.

One of the ways the IRS audits more tax returns with fewer people and in less time is by using computers. A very successful project initiated a few years ago is the Matching

Program. The IRS computers match interest and dividend information received from banks and brokerage firms with tax returns. For a long time, very few of the millions of Form 1099 information returns filed by the banks and other payors of interest and dividends were ever checked. These slips of paper were simply warehoused. Now, much of the 1099 information is supplied to the IRS on computer tapes instead of little pieces of paper. 1099's supplied by banks that still process them manually are likely to escape the IRS computers because of the sheer volume of forms involved. There is also an increased chance that the forms themselves may get lost. (For just these reasons, some people invest their money only at small "country" banks that do not have sophisticated computers.)

THE AUDIT LOTTERY

The audit lottery is a game played in the gray area of the tax code. There are many places where the law is not very clear or where court decisions are in conflict. There are even more situations in which neither the courts nor the IRS has ruled on a specific tax issue. The lottery comes into play when aggressive taxpayers or tax preparers take advantage of the gray areas by resolving doubts in their own favor, hoping to get away without being audited.

The audit lottery is still a viable game, with the odds in the taxpayer's favor. As long as there is a reasonable basis for the taxpayer's position, all the IRS can do is collect the tax that should have been paid, plus interest. Because the interest charged by the IRS is now pegged at the prime rate and is adjusted every six months, the advantage of receiving a low-interest loan from the government (if you are audited and have to pay back taxes) has been eliminated.

Since the chances of being audited are relatively small

--and if you are audited the IRS agent assigned to your case has to identify the tax issue in question and then develop it--many knowledgeable tax practitioners advise their clients to take a position favorable to themselves that can be reasonably argued under the law.

How Are Tax Returns Targeted for Audit?

Tax returns are selected for examination by a combination of computer and human factors. It is possible to improve the odds slightly against having your tax return selected by doing what the tax pros do for their own clients. Be aware, though, that there is nobody around (at least nobody who is talking) who knows the IRS computer program used to determine whose tax return is a candidate for audit.

What is public knowledge about the computer side of the selection process is that the computer determines the likelihood of a particular tax return generating additional tax dollars, if it is examined, by using a scoring system known as the Discriminant Income Function (DIF). Each tax return processed by the computer is assigned a DIF score. The higher the score, the more likely the return will be audited. The formula used to arrive at the DIF score is updated on a regular basis with information gathered by IRS examiners. Data is compiled from the thousands of tax returns actually audited, and the highly guarded and secret DIF formula is then modified. No public information is available on the factors that go into the DIF scoring.

Another scoring factor used by the IRS computers is known as Total Positive Income (TPI). TPI is the sum of all positive income values appearing on a return, with losses treated as zero. The purpose of this system is to eliminate or minimize the use of adjusted gross income as a factor in deciding the

potential for additional tax dollars if a return is audited.

The IRS found that it was not getting a true reading of tax returns when it relied on adjusted gross income. An adjusted gross income of, say, $15,000 can represent either a salary of $15,000 or a salary of $150,000 with tax shelters that bring the adjusted gross income down to $15,000. High-income taxpayers are less likely to escape audit now that the IRS computers have a second method to check for high audit potential.

The human process of tax return selection is much less scientific but just as important. After a tax return has been identified by the computer as having audit potential, it is shipped to the District Office and manually screened by the Classification Division. An IRS examiner assigned to the Classification Division gives most tax returns a quick "once over" to determine if the computer has made an obvious error in selecting it or if there is a special item to be brought to the attention of the examining agent ultimately assigned to the return.

If at this initial human level of contact there is adequate explanation or proof of a particular deduction attached to your return, the Classifier may decide that an audit is not in order. For example, receipts attached to your tax return that prove property was donated to a charity may satisfy the Classifier and eliminate the need for an audit to document the claims.

If your return reaches the Classifier at the end of the day, he or she may be bleary-eyed and less concerned about what you reported, and the special attention that might have been given to a particular issue will not be given. When your return actually reaches the Classifier is, of course, out of your control.

Knowing Average Deductions
Can Help Prevent an Audit

Some tax professionals attach great importance to the latest

statistics correlating deductions claimed with adjusted gross income, in an effort to determine the degree of risk of an audit their clients face. Recent numbers released by the IRS concerning personal income tax returns reflect only average amounts (Figure 1-2). An assumption is made that the computers use average numbers to determine if your particular tax deductions are likely to be disallowed if they are higher than average.

Income (Thousands)	Medical	Taxes	Charity	Interest
$20-25	1,544	1,791	734	3,016
$25-30	1,387	2,195	797	3,298
$30-40	1,405	2,690	900	3,778
$40-50	1,872	3,437	1,113	4,679
$50-75	2,741	4,711	1,553	6,259
$75-100	5,900	6,833	2,697	9,187
$100 or more	10,543	15,677	9,039	17,019

1-2. Average deductions based on adjusted gross income.

How to Reduce Your Chances of Being Audited

You may have the impression at this point in the discussion that the IRS computers are quite sophisticated and that it is virtually impossible to do anything legally to divert their eagle eye from your tax return. By and large this is true, but there are at least two things that may help minimize the effect of the IRS's high-tech capabilities.

First, how income is reported on the return may make a difference. Suppose you have freelance income. If it is merely reported as "Other Income" with an appropriate description as to its source, chances of having the return selected for audit may be smaller than if the same income is reported as business income on Schedule C (Income from a Sole Proprietorship).

Second, you can minimize your chances of being audited by filing as late as legally permissible. A tax return filed around April 15 generally has a greater chance of being audited

than one filed on October 15 (the latest possible date). This is because the IRS schedules audits more than a year in advance. As returns are filed and scored by the computer, local IRS districts submit their forecasted requirements for returns with audit potential. The fulfillment is made from returns already on hand. If your return is filed on October 15, there is a smaller chance that it will be among the returns shipped out to the District Office in the first batch. As a result of scheduling and budget problems that are likely to develop in the two years after your return has been filed, it may never find its way into the second batch slated for examination.

Although the IRS is wise to this ploy and has taken steps to make sure that the selection process is as fair as possible, inequities invariably result. Why not try to be part of the group that has the smallest chance of being audited?

The best way to reduce your chances of being audited is to avoid certain items universally thought to trigger special IRS scrutiny. There are also some common-sense considerations that should be thought about before you mail in your return. They are often overlooked by the very people who can least afford to be the subject of an audit. Here are a few examples:

Some people who are in cash businesses are not content with merely skimming some of their income. They also want to get every possible tax deduction--which is where the potential for audit comes in. When a business owner reports only a modest income, the IRS naturally becomes suspicious if that person also claims many business expenses and has high interest expense deductions. Two immediate questions are raised in the mind of the IRS examiner: Where does this person get money for personal living expenses and how is he or she able to make the principal repayments to justify the interest expense? When you are

preparing your return, step back and think like an IRS auditor. If you can spot questions, so can the IRS.

What else can be done to minimize the chances of being audited? The following items should be reviewed carefully:

- Choose your return preparer carefully. When the IRS suspects return preparers of incompetence or misconduct, it can force them to produce a list of all their clients--all of whom may face further IRS examination, regardless of their personal honesty.

- Avoid tax shelters. Many tax shelters are perfectly legitimate, but many have been identified by the IRS as abuses. If you really want to avoid any chance of an audit, steer clear of all but the most conservative tax-shelter investments.

- Avoid formal membership in barter clubs. Members of these clubs trade goods and services on a cashless basis. The club keeps track of all transactions between members. Although no cash changes hands, these trades are taxable like any other profitable deal. Very often, however, they are not reported to the IRS. The IRS can force such clubs to produce membership lists, so that the returns of all club members can be examined.

- Answer all questions on the return. IRS computers generally flag returns with unanswered questions. For example, there is a question asking if you maintain funds in a foreign bank account. Even if you do not, you should answer no to the question.

- Fill in the return carefully. A sloppy return may indicate a careless taxpayer. The IRS may examine the return to be sure the carelessness did not lead to any mistakes.

- Categorize each deduction. Don't place deductions under headings such as miscellaneous or sundry. If you can't categorize a deduction, the IRS may decide you can't prove it.

- Avoid round numbers. A deduction that's rounded off

to the nearest hundred or thousand dollars will raise IRS suspicions. It makes it look as though the taxpayer is guessing at the deduction's size, rather than determining it from accurate records.

• <u>Limit deductions for unreimbursed business expenses and casualty losses</u>. These deductions typically trigger audits. Try to have as many business expenses as possible reimbursed by your employer rather than taking them as tax deductions. It's cheaper for you and will not make your tax return stand out. Make sure that casualty losses can be properly documented and be aware that the IRS may be able to make a case that you actually realized a gain from the receipt of insurance proceeds, even though you think you had a loss. Insist that your tax advisor check this out carefully before taking a deduction.

• <u>Avoid filing amended returns that claim refunds</u>. The IRS gives special attention to amended tax returns, where people say they "forgot" to deduct something on the original return. Although your claim may be entirely legitimate, it opens up your entire tax return for examination. By the time the audit is over you could find yourself with a bill for additional taxes rather than a refund check. One way to avoid this problem is to file your amended tax return one week before the statute of limitations expires. This way, the most the IRS can do is disallow your claim for a refund. Since the statute of limitations will have expired by the time the IRS gets around to checking on the claim (and perhaps your entire return), it will not be able to get any more money from you.

Chapter 2
Cutting through
IRS Red Tape

There are ways to make the IRS bureaucracy work for you--and work quickly. The key is knowing where to call or write and what to say to get fast action.

Unclear Notices for Payment

One of the most frustrating experiences in dealing with the IRS is receiving a notice telling you that money is owed and you have no idea why. What compounds this feeling of frustration is that a new notice is received every few weeks, with more interest and penalty added to the unpaid balance. What should you do? Generally, it does little good to call the IRS because it is barred from giving information over the telephone. The best way to handle this is to send a letter asking for clarification to the IRS office immediately upon receiving a notice (the address appears on the notice). Keep a copy of the letter and obtain a mailing receipt. Each time the IRS sends a follow-up notice, send it a copy of your original letter with a short cover letter explaining that you have previously responded and are waiting for an answer. Keep a copy of all follow-up letters and mailing receipts.

IRS Mistakes

You may get a notice from the IRS that is clear enough but that is wrong. It is not a good idea to pay a bill from the IRS without checking it out first. Someone may have made a mistake at the IRS in screening your return, and this gave rise to the bill. The IRS

has an "Unallowable Items" program under which it disallows items that it deems unallowable (even against Tax Court decisions), without asking questions first. All the while, though, your deductions may be perfectly legitimate. Make sure you understand why the IRS wants more money before paying. If you can't figure it out, call your accountant or write to the IRS and request an explanation.

Another common IRS mistake that generates a bill requesting more money is IRS failure to post payments properly. Payments of estimated tax or other payments received during the year (with a tax return or with a request for an extension to file) may have been credited to another taxpayer's account. If you have evidence of making payments for which the IRS computer did not give you credit, send the IRS photocopies of the front and back of all checks in question, with a short note explaining that proper credit was not given.

Incorrect Refund Checks

Sometimes the IRS sends out refund checks in error (not on purpose, but it does happen). Eventually, it asks for the money back, with interest! if you receive a refund check made out to you, but you know that you are not entitled to it, don't keep it. Send back the check and ask for an explanation. Say that you don't want to accept the check unless an explanation is received. Keep copies of the check and your covering letter.

Uncooperative Employees

Because the IRS is such a large organization, it does have some employees who are not as efficient as they should be. Generally, though, the majority of the people working there, even at the clerical level, are competent and try hard to resolve problems.

If you feel that the person at the IRS who is responding

to your problem cannot handle it adequately or just doesn't want to be bothered, ask to speak to the person's immediate supervisor. If that doesn't work, ask to speak to that person's boss, and so on up the chain of command.

Problems Resolution Office

To its credit, the IRS has made significant progress in helping the public cut through the bureaucracy within the IRS. It has established a Problems Resolution Office to act as a liaison in an effort to resolve all of the problems (and others) discussed in this chapter.

　　To get the Problems Resolution Office working for you, you have to inform it that your efforts to resolve the problem through normal channels have been unsuccessful. Each IRS District Office and Service Center has a Problems Resolution Office. Try to submit as much information and relevant documentation as possible to the staffer assigned to your case since it will expedite matters.

Chapter 3
Surviving an IRS Audit

Very few things in this world have the effect of bringing the most hardened people to their knees the way notification of an IRS audit can. The letter from the IRS notifying a taxpayer that he or she has been selected for an audit contains language that is far from threatening, yet it strikes terror in the heart of most recipients. Various survival tactics can be used in preparing to do battle at the IRS audit. All of them are legal, but some aren't very nice.

Types of Audits

CORRESPONDENCE AUDIT

Some IRS audits are more thorough than others. The least thorough is a correspondence audit. Here, the IRS seeks to test compliance with perhaps one item on either a regional or national basis. For example, the IRS may send out hundreds of letters asking for verification of energy credit expenditures. On receipt of this notice, all you have to do is mail in the appropriate documentation to support your deduction.

Technically, this inquiry constitutes an audit. Once it takes place, there is very little chance that the rest of your return for that particular tax year will ever be audited. If the IRS should decide it wants to audit your return at a later date, it must go through a formal "reopening procedure"--which is rarely done. The obvious advantage of the correspondence audit is that if the IRS does not select an area in which you may be vulnerable, it will never know that it could have made other adjustments to your return that might have resulted in more tax.

OFFICE AUDIT

The next level of audit is the Office Audit. This examination is handled at a local IRS office. Typically, one or two deductions on your return will be questioned. Absent special circumstances, such as suspicion of fraud or gross errors in other areas of the return, the audit will not be extended to other issues. The primary advantage of the Office Audit is that it is generally conducted by individuals who lack the sophistication in tax matters needed to recognize more significant issues. The training and method of operation at the Office Audit level consists of telling the examiner (called a Tax Auditor) exactly what to look for in a given issue. The audit will be conducted mechanically and "by the book."

FIELD AUDITS

These are conducted by the best educated employees at the IRS, known as Revenue Agents. They are usually assigned the tax returns of businesses and wealthy individuals. An audit conducted by a Revenue Agent is usually quite complete, and although it will not examine every item in depth, it will attempt to cover many areas. One of the jobs of the Revenue Agent is to identify promptly areas with the potential for extra tax dollars and then to spend time developing the tax issues.

The chances of having the IRS uncover unreported income or disallowing deductions that are either personal or otherwise not deductible are more likely at the Field Audit than at any other type of IRS examination. It is unwise to try to handle a Field Audit yourself because the potential adverse ramifications can be severe--even if you think you did everything right! A sharp Revenue Agent can be quite creative when it comes to interpreting the Internal Revenue Code in the government's favor. Your ability to survive such creativity is enhanced by having an experienced practitioner representing your interests.

TCMP AUDIT

The most encompassing type of IRS audit is the TCMP Audit. TCMP stands for Taxpayer Compliance Measurement Program. TCMP audits are conducted to gain a statistical sample of the kinds of adjustments that are being uncovered. (For example, are adjustments of medical deductions on returns with an adjusted gross income of $25,000 or less more likely than on returns with an adjusted gross income of $100,000 or more?) The results of these audits are used to reprogram the IRS computers so that in the future they can select those returns most likely to result in additional tax dollars.

TCMP audits are usually conducted by Revenue Agents. The biggest problem with these examinations is that the Agent is required to comment on every item appearing on the tax return, starting with the spelling of your name. This does not mean that every line is audited, but the audit is lengthy and there is greater risk that adjustments will be found that will cost you a lot of money. One of the required audit techniques is the analysis of all a taxpayer's bank accounts for possible monies that were deposited but not reported.

CRIMINAL INVESTIGATIONS

These investigations, conducted by IRS employees known as Special Agents, are the most threatening to your personal liberty. The job of the Special Agent is to gather evidence of the commission of a tax crime. The least serious penalty that may result from a criminal investigation is the payment of some extra tax. The most serious penalty is indictment, conviction, and a jail sentence.

The anxiety created by a criminal investigation can be overwhelming. In most cases the subject of the investigation is not a "crook" or "Mafia" character. It is likely to be a profes-

sional or successful small businessperson who got carried away rationalizing that some of the money received during the year wasn't really income or, if it was income, that nobody would ever find out if it wasn't reported. The IRS gains tremendous publicity when a local person is convicted of tax evasion. As a result of an indictment or a conviction, the IRS assures itself that the level of voluntary compliance increases.

The subject of criminal investigations is so important that a whole chapter in this book (Chapter 10) is devoted to it.

Audit Survival Tactics

Knowing how the system at the IRS works gives an experienced practitioner an advantage when it comes to representing a client at an audit. Here are some of the truly "inside" things that go on.

POSTPONING APPOINTMENTS

It is possible, though not likely, that the IRS will actually change its mind about auditing you if you have postponed the appointment enough times. The IRS is constantly under pressure to start and finish tax examinations. If the return selected for an audit becomes "old" (i.e., more than two years have passed since the return was filed), the IRS may not want to start the audit. This situation may develop if you are notified of an audit about 15 to 16 months after filing. By the time you have cancelled one or two appointments, the 24-month cut-off period may have been reached.

When is the best time to cancel? The day before the appointment. By that time, the next available appointment will probably not be for 6 to 8 weeks.

TRANSFERRING THE AUDIT

If your accountant is located in another IRS district or is closer to another IRS office, request that your case be transferred to

that district or office. It may take the IRS up to three months to send your file to the second location. Sometimes, the new office may not even audit your return because of workload problems.

BEST TIME TO SCHEDULE AN AUDIT

To someone uninitiated, it may seem ridiculous that one time of the day or month is better than another to have your tax return audited. However, a real advantage can be gained by following some simple tips. Try to schedule an audit before a three-day weekend. The auditor may be less interested in the audit and more interested in the holiday. Another excellent time to schedule an appointment is at the end of the month. If an auditor has not "closed" enough cases that month, he or she may be inclined to go easy on you to gain a quick agreement and another closed case. As for the best time of the day, most pros like to start an audit at about 10 o'clock in the morning. By the time it comes to discussing adjustments with the auditor, it will be close to lunch time. If you are persistent, the auditor may be willing to make concessions just to get rid of you so as not to interfere with lunch plans.

BE PREPARED

The Boy Scout motto should be adhered to religiously. Be prepared to show the auditor, in a logical and easy-to-understand fashion, how you arrived at the numbers on your return. Back up everything on your workpaper with the appropriate documentation, be it a receipt, cancelled check, or something else. When documentation is not available, make sure the workpaper shows how you estimated the expenditure in question.

What about the "trick" of bringing all your receipts to the audit in a shopping bag? Unless you really know what you are doing, this is likely to backfire. For one thing, you have not established one ounce of credibility. For another, the auditor

will have an opportunity to look at more documents than he or she should. It will give the auditor an insight into your spending patterns and help determine what expenses may be questionable.

REQUESTS FOR OTHER TAX RETURNS

Sometimes, out of nothing more than curiosity, the auditor may ask to see your returns for the past year or two or even the returns filed after the return being audited. It is rarely a good idea to volunteer copies of these returns. If the auditor wants them badly enough, there is an internal procedure whereby he or she can get them. The procedure is cumbersome for the auditor and time-consuming. If the request is made, just say that you will have to look for the returns and get back to the auditor later. There is a good chance the question may not be raised again. If it is, just avoid answering it.

COOPERATION

It is generally a good idea to try to get the audit over as quickly as possible--so be cooperative. This does not mean that you should volunteer information not requested or answer questions not really asked. For example, a simple question like "Why did you deduct the cost of this dinner?" could be answered in any of the following ways:

1. Why do you want to know?   (least cooperative)

2. I discussed a potential business deal with Mr. Jones, who is my customer.   (cooperative)

3. I have been deducting the cost of business meals for years, even when the people I take out are only remotely related to my business. After all, I never know when one of them may become a customer. In fact, sometimes I don't even get a receipt.
   (overly cooperative)

INTIMIDATION

It is possible to intimidate the auditor by raising your voice or demanding to speak to a superior. This tactic should be used only in extreme cases, where the auditor is either unreasonable or nasty. Most employees at the IRS are usually pleasant and professional. Treat them nicely and they are likely to reciprocate.

UNPLEASANT WORKING CONDITIONS (FIELD AUDITS)

When an agent comes to your place of business to conduct an audit, there is no law that says that you must install him or her in the executive suite. A folding table in a room that is poorly lit and poorly ventilated is not really conducive to a long stay. The agent is likely to become uncomfortable and want to wrap up the audit as soon as possible.

Tactics That Never Should Be Used

- Never lie to or mislead an IRS employee. That is a crime!

- Never threaten an IRS employee even if he or she should threaten you first.

- Never attempt to bribe an IRS employee. In addition to being a crime, it simply doesn't accomplish anything. With the exception of probably less than 1/10 of 1 percent, IRS employees maintain the highest sense of integrity. Even a friendly offer of something of value (honestly not intended as a bribe) will make IRS employees apprehensive in trying to work out a settlement of your case. They are likely to feel they are being set up or tested by the IRS internal investigation division.

How to Deal with Special Problems During an Audit

Knowing what to say during an audit and then how you say it could mean the difference between getting yourself out of a sticky

situation or getting yourself into more trouble. Even the most routine audit could turn into a disaster if the wrong thing is said in response to a question or if the wrong type of documentation is supplied to support a position you have taken.

RESPOND CAREFULLY TO QUESTIONS

How much does the IRS really know about you before the audit starts? In most cases, very little or nothing. A smart agent will attempt to learn about you during the course of the audit by asking very personal questions. The purpose is to gain insight into how you earn your money, how you conduct your business, and what your standard of living is. All these facts are stored in the back of the agent's mind until something is said that may trigger them for possible use against you. Therefore, one way to avoid problems during an audit is to be careful about what you say in response to the agent's questions.

Let's say that the agent has asked you a question you do not want to answer. Don't say, "I will not answer that question!" Rather, say, "Why do you want to know that?" or, "I'll have to think about that and get back to you." Either get back to the agent with an answer or hope that the question won't be raised again.

LOST OR MISPLACED RECORDS

One special problem occurs in many audits when certain (or all) records have been misplaced, lost, or destroyed. Can you merely tell the IRS agent that the records are unavailable and therefore there can be no audit? You can, but if you do, it is likely that the agent will simply disallow the deductions for the unverified items. A better idea is to suggest an alternative audit approach.

One way is for the agent to audit the same item on a prior or subsequent year's return. If an adjustment is made, you agree to go along with a disallowance of the same amount (or same percentage) on the return where the records do not exist. Another way

is to suggest that the agent consider a specific period of time--say, 1 month--and you will reconstruct the records.

UNREPORTED INCOME

What do you do if you filed a tax return knowing that you didn't report all your income? If the agent should blatantly ask you if you reported all your income, you cannot lie and say "yes," since technically you will have committed a crime. If you say "no," you have taken a step toward incriminating yourself. The best way to respond is, "Do you have an indication that all of my income was not reported?" After an answer has been received, respond by saying, "I'll have to speak to my accountant and get back to you." At this point it is imperative that you attempt to wrap up the meeting and speak to an experienced tax attorney. Do not permit the agent to photocopy any records or transcribe any of your books. Come up with a reason why you can't continue the audit that day, and arrange for another date. Then let someone experienced take over as your representative.

DUBIOUS DEDUCTIONS

Suppose in preparing your tax return you include certain expenses that are probably not deductible or are, in fact, personal expenses that are definitely not deductible. The agent asks to look at these expenses. What do you do? It may be smart at this point to tell the agent just to disallow them. Showing the documentation for the items in question makes the credibility of your entire tax return suspect. But telling the agent to disallow the items increases the chances that some part of the deduction will be allowed.

How to Negotiate with a Revenue Agent

One of the "inside" things that most people don't know about the IRS (and which the IRS will never officially admit) is that almost

any issue can be negotiated. This doesn't mean that if the Revenue Agent assigned to your return has developed an excellent case for the government, the agent will concede all or part of it. It does mean that there is plenty of give and take between the Revenue Agents and knowledgeable tax practitioners who regularly represent clients before the IRS.

Why should Revenue Agents be willing to give up some of the adjustments proposed? There are two major reasons. One is that agents want you to agree with their findings because it makes their job easier if they simply issue one report that you will sign. Another reason is that agents know that not every item they propose to adjust will be sustained at the Appeals Division or in Tax Court. What some Revenue Agents do is actually propose more adjustments than they know they should in an effort to create leverage for themselves when it comes to bargaining. They are likely to give in on those issues they know ultimately can't be won by the government.

One of the best techniques to use when negotiating with a Revenue Agent is to try to formulate some rationale the agent can use to support the proposed adjustments. The rationale, which you can help to develop, makes it easier for the agent to agree to your counterproposals. He or she may be concerned that the Review Staff, which monitors completed audits for quality control purposes, may take exception if the explanation given is inadequate.

Example: John Jones, the taxpayer, is a traveling salesman, who has just completed an audit with a Revenue Agent. The agent proposes to disallow the deduction claimed by Jones for taxicabs since Jones had no receipts to support his deduction. The way to negotiate with the agent is to say one (or all) of the following:

1. I'll agree with everything you propose, but I want you to allow me something for taxicabs.

2. I'll agree with everything you propose, but I just can't go along with a total disallowance for taxicabs. It's reasonable that I took at least two taxicabs each week at $4.00 a trip. That's $8 a week for 50 weeks. Allow me $400 and I'll sign your report right now.

3. Your report is totally wrong! How can you say that I don't take taxicabs? Do you think I walk around the city? I have customers everywhere. I want you to allow me half the deduction I claimed or I'll go to the Appeals Division. They'll probably allow me more than half!

In each answer above, note that John Jones has not insisted on the entire deduction he claimed for taxicabs. Since no receipts or other documents were provided to support the deduction, it would be unreasonable for Jones to insist that the agent allow everything claimed.

Jones's answers make it possible for the Revenue Agent to allow part of the deduction rather than disallowing it entirely.

What to Do When You're Audited and You Don't Have Receipts

Many people, unfortunately, have spent money for tax deductible items but have lost the receipts or never asked for them in the first place. If you're never audited, it doesn't matter that some receipts are missing. But what do you do when you are audited and the auditor will not take your word that you actually spent the money?

Not having receipts can be a sore point, particularly at an audit involving cash outlays for contributions and travel and entertainment. Not having receipts is also a problem when it comes to valuation of property for a casualty loss claim or when the property is donated to a charity.

Under the law, you are required to keep a diary or account book and record the time, place, amount, and business purpose of each expenditure as you make it. Receipts are required for any item over $25. As a practical matter the IRS may allow your deduction (at least in part) if you can reconstruct your expenses and come up with reasonable evidence to corroborate them. But it doesn't have to.

OUT-OF-TOWN TRIPS

It is possible to reconstruct expenses incurred on out-of-town trips in the following manner. First, bring evidence from your employer or the people you dealt with to show why you made the trip. To prove train or plane fare, the rules require a receipt, but a statement from your travel agent that you purchased tickets should be sufficient. If you didn't use a travel agent and paid cash at the airline counter, ask the airline to provide you with a statement showing what the fare was at the time of the trip. It is possible to support lodging costs by showing the agent a cancelled check along with the hotel's rate card.

Living expenses while away from home are harder to prove. Try to reconstruct how much you spent each day for meals, tips, cabs, telephone, and laundry. A total figure for the whole trip will probably not be acceptable.

BUSINESS ENTERTAINMENT

Even if you have receipts and can prove your expenses to the penny, you still have to show whom you entertained, your business relationship to that person, and the business purpose. If you entertained at home but have no receipts, reconstruct your expenses by making a list of all guests and your business relationship to them, what you bought for the occasion, where you bought everything, and how much you spent. Other evidence could be photographs, invitations, and thank-you notes received from guests.

The more details you furnish, the more likely the agent will allow a reasonable deduction.

CONTRIBUTIONS

The IRS does not really expect a receipt for out-of-pocket cash contributions made on a weekly basis--as long as the amount is not unreasonable. What do you do if you really give a significant amount of money, in cash, to your church or synagogue each week? At the least, be prepared to show the IRS a letter from a person in authority at your place of worship attesting to the fact that you attend services each week and that the person knows you to be generous.

CASUALTY LOSSES

A casualty loss arising from a fire, theft, or accident is usually easy to prove from police or fire records and insurance reports. Proving the amount of the loss can sometimes be difficult because you are usually required to verify your basis (cost) in the destroyed property, which may have been acquired years ago.

To verify the cost of something acquired a long time ago, it may be possible to obtain insurance records or appraisals made at the time of purchase if the original receipt is lost. A statement from a knowledgeable person as to what the item would have cost at the time it was acquired is better than nothing. If inherited property is the subject of a casualty loss, the best proof of its value is the value assigned to it for estate tax purposes.

Tax Shelter Audits: How Do You Deal with Them?

Over the last few years, many people have invested in tax shelters, sometimes without even really knowing exactly what they were investing in. Let's say you are one of them. Tax

deductions are claimed and the matter is forgotten. Suddenly the IRS, which has been devoting substantial resources to examining tax shelters, enters the picture and informs you that the movie deal that saved you $20,000 in taxes a few years ago is being audited. Worse still, the IRS tells you that when the audit is completed, you will be entitled to only a $2,000 tax savings--not the $20,000 you claimed!

This scenario occurs with regularity to many people. Unfortunately, it is a tax shelter trap they learn about the hard way.

Since tax shelters are typically organized as limited partnerships, the investor is the limited partner, but the general partner controls the manner in which the business is conducted. Accordingly, the general partner is the person responsible for conducting the audit and financing the cost of appeals. The investor has very little to do with the ultimate outcome of the audit. The only involvement may be a request to contribute money to a special defense fund to fight the IRS. If the IRS decides on an audit, be prepared to pay a lot of money to fight the issue in court.

What do you do if your tax shelter deduction is being threatened and the general partner or the promoter of the tax shelter is out of town or, worse, out of business? What happens if the general partner doesn't want to incur the expense of fighting the IRS? Since the cost of litigating a tax shelter case is very expensive, it is impossible for any individual partner to fight the IRS. The only option you have is to threaten to sue the general partner if he or she does not finance the litigation.

The IRS generally allows an investor a deduction equal to the actual cash put into the deal, if it disallows the benefits claimed--benefits such as investment tax credits or various tax deductions the shelter promised.

Chapter 4
Fighting the IRS
on Its Own Turf

If your tax return is selected for an audit, you may be unable to reach an agreement with the examiner on whether additional tax should be assessed. The disagreement may be over a matter of law--whether a particular law should be interpreted as the government suggests; over a matter of fact--did you really spend $100 to entertain a business client; or over both. Fortunately, the IRS Appeals Division has a procedure to handle such disputes.

The employees of the Appeals Division are experienced examiners whose job is to render a second opinion on the merits of your case and the case developed by the examiner. This second opinion should not be considered an impartial review--because it is not. If the examiner has taken a position consistent with current IRS policies and the facts in the case justify that position, the Appeals Division will sustain the examiner's findings. You will have to go to Tax Court (the subject of Chapter 5) if you are not willing to pay the tax. As a practical matter, the Appeals Division encourages settlements and compromises.

Traps and Benefits of Going to the Appeals Division

The most significant trap a taxpayer must be aware of before deciding to appeal the proposed adjustments is the ability of the Appeals Division to increase those adjustments. At the Appeals Division level, new issues that could result in additional tax may be raised.

If it is obvious that the examining agent missed a sig-

nificant tax issue, there is good reason to forego your opportunity to appeal. It may be better strategy to do nothing, in which case a Notice of Deficiency* will be issued, permitting you to go to Tax Court.

Just as there may be a trap in going to the Appeals Division, there may also be a benefit. The Appeals Division is vested with "settlement authority," which means it can close cases without regard to the tax law. An example of the use of settlement authority occurs when two people each claim the same dependent. The Appeals Division can split the exemption and allow $500 to each taxpayer.

The examining agent is technically not permitted to be concerned about the "hazards of litigation" (the term the government uses to describe a situation in which it may lose a particular issue if the case goes to court). The Appeals Division takes this into consideration in determining how much of an offer it should make to a taxpayer for settlement. The IRS often lets a taxpayer get away without paying additional taxes if that will prevent an unfavorable court precedent from being established that would be used by thousands of other taxpayers.

Assuming no new issues are raised, there is almost always a chance of a compromise on some part of the proposed adjustments at the Appeals Division--even if it only amounts to 10 percent.

How to Appeal Audit Results to the IRS Appeals Division

If agreement is not reached at the audit level, you will be notified in writing of your right to appeal the proposed adjustments.

---

*The form issued by the IRS that officially puts you on notice of its determination that more tax is owed. See "How to Take Your Own Case to the U.S. Tax Court--Small Case Division" in Chapter 5.

This notice is commonly refered to as a "30 Day Letter," which means that an appeal must be filed within 30 days of the date of the letter.

A formal written protest must be filed in all cases, except where the proposed adjustment does not exceed $2,500 or where the audit was conducted at the Office or Correspondence level. It is a good idea to send a formal written request to the Appeals Division even if it is technically not required so that your disagreement is officially on record.

The formal protest can be prepared quite simply. Here is an example:

[Date]

District Director
120 Church Street
New York, N.Y. 10008

Re: Robert Smith
1985-1040
123-33-4890

AU:F 30 D

Dear Sir:

This is a formal written appeal of the findings of the examining officer. A copy of the examiner's report is enclosed. I request that this matter be considered by the Appeals Division.

The following adjustment has been proposed to which exception is taken:

Casualty Loss $4,900

Statement of Facts

[Set forth the facts that support your position.]

1. On January 8, 1985 my automobile was stolen. A police report was filed, as well as a claim with my insurance company.

2. The car was purchased in 1981 for a total cost of $10,000

and was worth $5,000 at the time of the theft. No insurance proceeds were received as there was no coverage for theft.

<u>Statement of Law</u>

[Set forth the law or other authority on which you are relying.]

The Internal Revenue Code provides that a deduction be allowed for a casualty loss.

Under the penalty of perjury, I declare that I have examined the statement of facts presented in this protest and in any accompanying schedules and statements and, to the best of my knowledge and belief, they are true, correct, and complete.

Sincerely,

Robert Smith

How to Negotiate with an Appeals Officer

Depending upon the facts and circumstances, it may be easier to negotiate with the Appeals Officer than it was with the original examiner. The Appeals Division stresses to its employees that it wants cases settled at the Appeals level. The leverage you have is the option to take the fight to the Tax Court. The Appeals Division recognizes that if this happens it means more time and effort for the government.

The discussions with the Appeals Division should be approached with the attitude that you are willing to compromise if the settlement is fair. Although it is of course possible for the Appeals Division to reverse the examiner in all respects, it is unlikely that this will happen unless the examiner grossly misapplied the law.

Try to be creative in the negotiations to reduce the

proposed adjustment. To be really effective you need the services of an accountant. Many areas of the tax law are poorly defined and unsupported by precedent. Use this to your advantage. Try to give the Appeals Division employee something substantial to justify your position.

Chapter 5
Taking Your Tax Case
to Court

What do you do if you just cannot convince anyone at the IRS of the merits of your case? Do you have to give up and pay the extra tax just because a Revenue Agent thinks you underpaid? Fortunately, there is a last resort--the Tax Court, an independent judicial body not associated with the Internal Revenue Service.

Using the Tax Court as a Negotiating Tactic

In most cases, going to court costs more in legal fees than it is worth--even if you win the case. However, when it comes to fighting the IRS in Tax Court, the expense can be minimized. Underlying this is the idea that you will never actually have your case heard by a judge. You will agree to a compromise on the amount you owe the IRS before trial.

After a Tax Court petition (the form necessary to start the proceeding--more about this below) has been filed, your case is assigned to an attorney representing the IRS. He or she will contact you in an effort to resolve the case before trial. Because the IRS generally wants to settle as many cases as possible before trial (Rev. Proc. 82-42), you may even find that the IRS attorney will send your case back to the Appeals Division for further consideration. This is the division that disagreed with your position the first time around. Now it's likely to listen more carefully.

Suddenly you find that the IRS is doing the best it can to reach a reasonable compromise. This is quite different from

the scenario before the filing of the Tax Court petition, when the IRS was probably telling you it had to be its way or not at all.

Why has there been such a change of heart at the IRS? Has some higher authority determined that the IRS has made a terrible mistake and justice must be served by reviewing your case again? Not exactly. What has happened is that by filing your Tax Court petition you have become one of literally tens of thousands of backlogged cases. Neither the court nor the IRS has the time, resources, or energy to bring every disputed tax case to a full-blown trial. Hence the effort to compromise.

THE ART OF COMPROMISE

Remember, a compromise doesn't mean that you will walk away from the IRS audit without having to pay anything. You will just pay less (and be charged less interest) than was originally requested. This will be the result if there really is some merit to the government's position and you can't prove everything that has been challenged. If your case is entirely without merit, the chances of a compromise are slim. Likewise, if the IRS case can't be substantiated, the IRS attorney assigned to the case will recognize the inherent weaknesses and reverse the findings of the examiner.

Take a typical situation. You think you are 100 percent correct, but can't prove it. Such a situation is likely to develop when travel and entertainment deductions have been challenged because the documentation to verify the deductions was inadequate. You know you really did spend the money for the business purpose you claim, but you just forgot to get a receipt. Even if you are right and the IRS is wrong, it still may be a good idea to consider a compromise. Justice is not always served in the courtroom--for reasons of time, work pressure, or perhaps the judge just doesn't like the way you look.

How to Take Your Own Case to the
U.S. Tax Court—Small Case Division

Although it is never a good idea to be your own lawyer--especially
when it comes to intricate tax law--it is indeed possible to represent yourself in the U.S. Tax Court if you elect to follow what
is known as the small tax case procedure. This election is possible if the Notice of Deficiency (the form issued by the IRS that
formally puts you on notice of its determination that more tax is
owed) indicates that $10,000 or less for any one year is due. Tech-
nically, you can still use the special small tax case procedure
even if the amount on the Notice of Deficiency is greater than
$10,000, as long as the amount you wish to contest is $10,000 or
less.

The procedure to follow to get into court is relatively
simple. A Tax Court Petition (see Appendix) must be filed with the
Tax Court within 90 days (not 3 months) of the date the Notice of
Deficiency was mailed to you by the IRS. For the petition to be
considered filed timely, it must actually be received by the Tax
Court within the 90-day period or it must be received in an enve-
lope with a U.S. postmark (not a postage meter imprint) showing a
legible date within the 90-day period. If the petition is late by
even 1 day, the court will not be allowed to hear your case.

At the time of filing, a $60 fee must accompany your pe-
tition. In addition to filing the petition, you should also file a
form requesting a place for trial. The court hears cases in each
state, and in many states there is more than one city in which a
case can be argued. Both the petition form and the request for
place of trial form are available by writing to the Tax Court, 400
Second Street, N.W., Washington, D.C. 20217. An instruction
booklet is also available from the same address.

The trial in a small tax case procedure is conducted

informally because the court acknowledges that the majority of litigants are unfamiliar with courtroom procedures. Testimony will be recorded and documents will be received in evidence. You may argue your case orally, in writing, or both. The decision rendered at the small tax procedure is final and cannot be appealed either by you or the IRS. A decision by the regular Tax Court can be appealed.

Choosing the Right Court

If the amount of extra tax the government wants is substantial, it is important that you know the options available to you.

1. Not to pay the tax and file a petition with the U.S. Tax Court.

2. Pay the tax, then file a claim for refund. If your claim is denied, you can then bring suit against the IRS in the District Court or the U.S. Claims Court.

One of the most unusual aspects of tax litigation in the United States is that with the same facts, each of the courts empowered to hear a tax case (Tax Court, District Court, or U.S. Claims Court) may reach a different decision. Therefore, taking advantage of "forum shopping" may be vital to your chances of winning. Forum shopping means reviewing decisions rendered by the various courts on issues similar to yours and then selecting the court (forum) that has ruled favorably for the taxpayer. The taxpayer is the party that can select the court to hear an action.

Most tax litigants choose the Tax Court, not because it may have favorable precedents but because the taxpayer is not first required to pay the tax the IRS says is owed. Because most people don't have the money on hand the IRS claims is owed or just don't want to part with it, the Tax Court is the most popular forum.

In Tax Court there is an unusual twist. The judge hearing your case may not be the person who decides the outcome. The presiding judge hears the case and writes an opinion, which is sent to the Chief Judge of the Tax Court for review. If the Chief Judge feels that the case is important or has unusual precedent-setting value, it will be submitted to all the judges of the Tax Court (18 judges) for a vote. The entire court will not necessarily decide the same way as the judge who first heard your case.

Cases heard in all of the courts can be appealed to the appropriate circuit of the Court of Appeals and to the Supreme Court.

The Odds of Settling

Unless your case is absolutely very weak, the odds of a settlement before trial are excellent. As discussed earlier in this chapter, IRS attorneys are overburdened and understaffed. Accordingly, any reasonable solution you propose will be considered.

Negotiating with IRS Lawyers

An experienced tax attorney should be retained to negotiate a settlement with the IRS. You stand a greater chance of having your offer considered seriously if someone experienced is doing the talking for you. Even if your attorney is retained only for negotiation and not for trial, it will be money well spent. The IRS attorney knows that you don't really know how to argue effectively in court (even in a small tax case procedure), so without your own attorney you are giving the IRS leverage.

In addition to routine job pressures, the IRS attorney fighting your case will be weighing other factors before deciding whether to compromise at all, and to what extent. One is the "hazards of litigation." What this means is that the IRS may be concerned that if it fights you in court and loses, your case will

establish unfavorable precedent. The importance of not setting unfavorable precedent gives the IRS an incentive to agree to a compromise out of court--even if it means letting you get away with tax which it thinks really should be paid. Other typical concerns of IRS lawyers are the relative merits of your case and theirs and the estimated amount of time it will take to prepare the case for trial.

Experience indicates that the best time to talk about compromise is as soon as the case is assigned to the IRS attorney. Once the attorney has invested a considerable amount of time in preparing the case for trial, added factors, such as a decision that your case has excellent precedential value for the government, may inhibit a settlement by the IRS.

Using the Tax Court Strategy Early On

Your ability to have your case heard by the Tax Court--and your knowledge of the procedure--can be used throughout the entire audit process as a negotiating tactic. At the initial audit level, where all the troubles start, let the examiner know that you feel that the proposed adjustments are wrong and that you intend to appeal the determination all the way to the Tax Court, regardless of cost (which in reality may be quite minimal). Although the examining agent may be less impressed with such a statement than would a member of the Appeals Division, it will still make an impression. You may be lucky enough to convince the agent that you are very serious about the position you have taken and about your credibility. This may cause the agent to reconsider the proposed adjustments.

The identical statement made at the Appeals Division is likely to carry more weight because if you go through with your "threat," the agent may get the case back again--this time with instructions to try to reach a compromise.

Chapter 6
Protecting Yourself with a Private Letter Ruling from the IRS

The IRS gives free audit insurance. By following a relatively simple procedure it is possible to obtain a ruling in advance of a contemplated tax transaction. If the facts set forth in your request for a ruling are identical with the facts of the transaction and if nothing has been left out of your request, the IRS will not change its mind if you are audited later on. It is generally wise to request a private letter ruling if the consequences of a particular transaction would be seriously damaging to you if you and the IRS don't see eye to eye.

As a matter of IRS procedure, a private letter ruling issued to one taxpayer cannot be relied on by another taxpayer, even if the factual situation is similar or identical. In practice, though, a favorable ruling issued to another taxpayer does provide valuable insight into the position the IRS will take if you are audited.

When to Ask for a Ruling and When Not To

Ask for a ruling:

• When the tax law requires you get a ruling--for example, in certain tax-free transactions involving foreign corporations.

• When you believe the law is in your favor and a major transaction hinges on favorable tax treatment.

• When the law is not clear or when you can't find a pos-

itive statement supporting your view in the law, the regulations, the public rulings, or in court decisions.

Don't ask for a ruling:

• If it seems likely that the ruling will not be favorable. You can proceed with the transaction without a ruling. If your return is not audited, the transaction will never be examined. A private letter ruling may act as a red flag to the IRS since a copy of the ruling must be attached to your tax return. The IRS is likely to audit you to make sure you actually did what you said you were going to do when it issued the ruling.

Issues the IRS Will
Not Rule On

The following are examples of issues the IRS will not rule on in advance:

• How estate taxes will apply to the property of a living person.

• Hypothetical transactions--i.e., transactions that have not yet taken place.

• Questions of fact. For example: Is this executive's compensation reasonable? What is the value of this piece of property?

• Requests from trade associations for rulings on how the law may affect members.

• Issues involving court decisions the IRS hasn't decided whether to accept or appeal.

• Issues involving tax code sections for which no final regulations have been put into effect (unless a business emergency makes a private letter ruling essential).

How to Get a Ruling

There is no special form to use when requesting a private letter ruling. Your letter should be addressed to the IRS, Asst. Commissioner (Technical), Att: T:FP:T, 1111 Constitution Avenue, N.W., Washington, D.C. 20224.

To speed things up, call the IRS in advance and state the general area of the ruling request. You will be given a code number to add to the address, which will direct the request to the individual in charge of rulings in that area.

Provide the following information in the letter:

• A statement of all the facts concerning the proposed transaction.

• An explanation of the transaction's business purpose.

• A statement of legal points and authorities in support of the requested ruling.

• A specific statement of what ruling you are asking for.

Include a request for a conference (if the IRS denies your request). Also include a statement that lists the identifying details that must be deleted when the ruling is made public. All private letter rulings requested after October 31, 1976, have been released to the public with names and identifying details omitted. By specifically telling the IRS the details you want omitted, there is less of a chance that something will become public record that could identify you.

Don't Rely on Someone Else's Ruling

As mentioned earlier, you can't technically rely on someone else's ruling when contemplating the pros and cons of a particular course of action. Another's ruling does, however, provide

valuable insight into the position the IRS may take if you are audited. Remember, though, another person's ruling may be revoked or superseded by the IRS, and you may never know about it--until it's too late. The IRS has no obligation to tell you of the change. Before embarking on a course of action, make sure that the ruling you are relying on is still in accord with IRS policy--by checking existing Revenue Rulings, subsequent rulings, and IRS Regulations.

Chapter 7
IRS Interest Rules

If you are audited and owe the IRS extra tax, you will be charged interest. The interest starts from the time the tax return being audited was originally due. For example, suppose you filed your 1985 tax return on March 18, 1986. If you are audited sometime in 1987 and owe an extra tax, the interest will start from April 15, 1986--the due date of the tax return.

Interest Rates from 1939 to 1986

Under current law, the IRS must adjust its interest rate semiannually to conform to the average prime rate. The new rate applies to tax underpayments, overpayments, and estimated penalties. Figure 7-1 shows the changes in IRS interest rates over the past 47 years.

From	To	Rate percent
1939	June 30, 1975	6
July 1, 1975	January 31, 1976	9
February 1, 1976	January 31, 1978	7
February 1, 1978	January 31, 1980	6
February 1, 1980	January 31, 1982	12
February 1, 1982	December 31, 1982	20
January 1, 1983	June 30, 1983	16
July 1, 1983	December 31, 1984	11
January 1, 1985	June 30, 1985	13
July 1, 1985	December 31, 1985	11
January 1, 1986	June 30, 1986	10

7-1. IRS interest rates since 1939.

Before 1983, interest on deficiencies and refunds was computed as simple interest. Starting January 1, 1983, interest is compounded daily.

Cash Bond Procedure

Some taxpayers being audited may feel there is a good chance they

will ultimately lose on some of the Revenue Agent's proposed adjustments. They may still want to take a shot at fighting the disallowance in Tax Court.

Problem: How can you pay the tax you may owe and at the same time avoid interest from accruing while your case is being processed by the IRS? The IRS has established Revenue Procedure 82-51, which permits a taxpayer to make a deposit to be applied against a potential tax liability so that interest will not accrue. The deposit must be made before the IRS sends a statutory notice of deficiency (90-day letter). When the money is sent to the IRS, it must be accompanied by a written request indicating that the payment is a "deposit in the nature of a cash bond."

There are some drawbacks to the procedure:

• No interest is paid on the money sent in as a cash bond if you win in Tax Court.

• The deposit is usually returned upon request, unless another tax liability is owed. You may not want to pay the other liability, but now the IRS has your money.

• No tax deduction is allowed for interest paid by posting a cash bond because technically there was no tax assessment to create the interest liability.

Chapter 8
Tax Compliance: Penalties
and Excuses

The Internal Revenue Code contains a host of penalties the IRS may
assess in an effort to encourage compliance with its rules and
regulations. Enactment of the Economic Recovery Tax Act of 1981
(ERTA) and the Tax Equity and Fiscal Responsibility Act of 1982
(TEFRA) has produced a considerable increase in the size (in dollars) of penalties already on the books (to adjust for inflation)
and in the addition of many new penalties designed to help the IRS
clean up areas in which civil adjustments were not adequate
enough to encourage compliance. The thrust of the new penalties,
is against people who invest in tax shelters or otherwise claim
deductions based on overvaluation of assets.

The most commonly assessed penalties are the penalties
for filing a late return and the penalties for paying tax late.

Penalties for Late Filing

The penalty for failure to file a tax return on time is the lesser
of $100 or 100 percent of the tax due (if the failure to file con-
tinues for more than 60 days from the due date of the tax return,
including extensions). If, for example, you are required to file
your personal tax return on April 15, don't file until July 15,
and don't bother (or forget) to ask for an extension, the penalty
will be 100 percent of the tax owed. If you owe no tax and are due a
refund, the penalty will be $100.

Penalties for Late Payment

The penalty for failure to pay tax on time is one-half of 1 percent

of the tax due, for each month it remains unpaid, up to a maximum of 25 percent. If you file your return up to 60 days late and also owe money (for which you will be assessed the failure-to-pay penalty), there is a special break. The amount of the failure-to-file penalty will be reduced by the amount of the failure-to-pay penalty. However, if you filed more than 60 days late, the failure-to-file penalty will not be reduced at all.

SUMMARY OF PENALTIES

If you file late and owe no money, the penalty is $100. If you file late and owe money, the failure-to-file penalty is the lesser of $100 or 100 percent of the tax due (if the return is filed more than 60 days late), and the failure-to-pay penalty is one-half of 1 percent of the tax due, for each month it remains unpaid, up to a maximum of 25 percent.

Penalty Appeals Procedure

What happens after the IRS informs you it has assessed a penalty? If you feel you have "reasonable cause" and that the penalty should not have been assessed, write to the IRS and inform it of the basis of your contention.

(What you feel is "reasonable cause" may not agree with the IRS definition. Reasonable cause is a loosely defined concept generally determined by the facts and circumstances of a given situation.)

The IRS maintains a special Penalty Appeals procedure that enables a taxpayer to contest a denial of a request for abatement of penalty. When you write to the IRS and explain your case, end the letter with the sentence: "It is requested that in the event of an unfavorable determination of my request for the abatement of the aforementioned penalties, this letter be forwarded to the Penalty Appeals Officer for reconsideration."

Excuses That Work

Suppose you filed your tax return late and did not obtain an extension. Worse still, you also owe the IRS money. The IRS has sent you a bill for the tax you owe plus interest and penalties. You know that the tax and interest must be paid but feel that you have "reasonable cause" for filing your return late. Fortunately, most IRS personnel will abate penalties if you present them with what they want to hear (it has to be the truth, though).

The following excuses work:

1. Death or serious illness of the taxpayer or a death or serious illness in the immediate family. In the case of failure to pay a penalty, the death or serious illness must be of an individual having the sole authority to make payment.

2. Destruction of the taxpayer's place of business or business records by fire or other disaster.

3. Unavoidable absence of the taxpayer from home or business.

4. Inability to obtain records necessary to determine the amount of tax due, for reasons beyond the taxpayer's control.

5. The facts indicate that the taxpayer's ability to pay has been materially impaired by civil disturbances.

6. The taxpayer is in a combat zone.

7. The taxpayer has exercised ordinary business care and prudence in providing for payment of taxes and has posted a bond or acceptable security, coupled with a collateral agreement showing that inability to pay the tax when due (or payment on the due date) would have caused undue hardship.

8. Any other reason showing that the taxpayer exercised ordinary care and prudence but still was unable to pay the tax when due.

9. Seasonal changes resulting in sudden increases in

the liability of a taxpayer not ordinarily required to make deposits. (This excuse applies to penalties for late payment or nonpayment of payroll taxes.)

10. Failure to file a tax return upon the advice of a reputable accountant or attorney whom the taxpayer selected with reasonable and ordinary prudence and who was furnished in good faith with information the taxpayer reasonably believed was sufficient.

11. Late filing by tax preparer. When a taxpayer has relied on an accountant or attorney to prepare a tax return, which was then not filed on a timely basis, the IRS usually allows this as an acceptable excuse. Technically, such an excuse is not reasonable cause, but it usually works, particularly when the accountant or attorney admits blame to the IRS in writing.

12. Absence of key employees. When a business has had heavy employee turnover or when an important financial executive such as a vice-president or controller is no longer employed by the business, it can be considered reasonable cause for late filing and late payment.

13. Change of CPA firm. If you recently fired a CPA firm because it was not taking care of things properly and on time and the problem wasn't discovered until new accountants were retained, it may be reasonable cause to abate a penalty.

14. Lost or misplaced records. This usually works if the information needed to prepare the tax return in question was misfiled or lost and had to be reconstructed.

Excuses That Don't Work

1. "I didn't pay the tax because I didn't have any money."

2. "I used the payroll taxes to run my business and keep 15 people employed."

3. "I don't know anything about taxes. I leave it all to my accountant."

4. "I didn't file the tax return because I thought I didn't have to file."

Remember, the easiest time to get the IRS to abate a penalty is when taxes have been outstanding for some time and you offer to pay up, in complete settlement, if all or part of the penalties are abated. The standard of reasonable cause now mysteriously becomes much less stringent.

Penalty for Substantial Understatement of Income Tax

TEFRA introduced a new penalty--10 percent of the amount of an "underpayment" attributable to a "substantial understatement" of income tax. An understatement is the difference between the tax shown on the return as originally filed and the correct tax. An understatement is substantial if it is greater than $5,000 ($10,000 for personal holding companies and corporations) and 10 percent of the tax actually due.

Example: John Jones files a return showing $3,000 in taxes due. After an audit by the IRS, the correct tax is determined to be $9,000. In this case the underpayment is $6,000, which is greater than the $5,000 test, and also more than 10 percent of the tax actually due. John Jones could be faced with a penalty of $600 (10 percent of the $6,000 underpayment) for substantial understatement of income tax.

There are three ways this penalty can be avoided:

1. REASONABLE CAUSE

The IRS can waive the penalty if the taxpayer can establish reasonable cause for the understatement and show that he or she acted in good faith. For example, if the understatement was created

because the taxpayer erroneously believed he or she was entitled to use income averaging, but really couldn't because of a technicality, the penalty could be waived.

2. SUBSTANTIAL AUTHORITY

In cases not involving tax shelters, the penalty may be avoided if the understatement resulted from the IRS's disallowing/ adjusting an item supported by the "substantial authority" the taxpayer relied upon. Proposed Regulations issued by the IRS define "authority" as including statutes, treaties, judicial opinions, Treasury Regulations, published Revenue Rulings and Procedures, and congressional intent as reflected in committee reports and statements of managers. "Authority" does not include opinions expressed in law review articles, opinion letter rulings, and technical advice.

It should be noted that a lawyer's unsupported opinion that a particular position is defensible, or even that it is correct, will not protect a taxpayer from the penalty.

3. DISCLOSURE

In cases not involving tax shelters, the penalty can be avoided if the taxpayer makes adequate disclosure of the facts surrounding the tax treatment of an item on the return. The Proposed Regulations require that a separate sheet be attached to the tax return with the following information:

a) A statement identifying the disclosure as an IRC section 6661 disclosure.

b) Identification of the item.

c) Amount of the item.

d) Either a description of the facts sufficient to apprise the IRS of the legal issue or a description of the legal issue.

Placing a disclosure notice on your tax return is like saying to the IRS, "Please audit me!" So be certain that you are ready and willing to be audited before you decide to make the disclosure.

Special rules are applicable to tax shelters. As an investor in a limited partnership you can be subject to the substantial-understatement-of-income-tax penalty if adjustments made to the partnership tax return flow down to your own return, if the resulting underpayment on your return meets the criteria discussed earlier in this chapter.

When it comes to tax shelter cases, a taxpayer cannot avoid the penalty simply by making a disclosure. Where a tax shelter exists, the "substantial authority" test must be met, as well as a subjective "more likely than not" test. The "more likely than not" standard means that the taxpayer must have believed that the tax deduction taken would be upheld. Typically, this subjective standard can be used if the taxpayer relies in good faith on a professional opinion that explicitly addresses the "more likely than not" issue.

It's worth noting that in a tax shelter case, an opinion that is silent on the "more likely than not" test will probably not hold up if the taxpayer wants to use it as an excuse.

Chapter 9
Owing Money to the IRS

After the IRS has made an assessment, you have 10 days to pay it in full or be subject to collection action. The Collection Division at the IRS has the responsibility of collecting delinquent accounts. Although an account is technically delinquent after 10 days, no one will show up at your door on the eleventh day. A series of threatening notices will be mailed to you, and eventually you will be contacted in person by a Revenue Officer.

What Power Does the IRS Have?

Can you merely tell the Revenue Officer that you can't pay the tax right now? Can you avoid seeing or speaking to the officer altogether? You can, but it really will not do you any good. Unlike other creditors, who must go to court to obtain a judgment against you and then go back to court to have that judgment enforced, the IRS need never go to court. The IRS is vested with the power to seize your property without a court order. The only requirement is that it have a valid assessment, give notice with a demand for payment (which has to be sent to your last known address), and give notice of intent to seize.

In addition to seizing your property, the IRS can also place a levy on your bank accounts and on your salary. This means that both your bank and your employer must turn over to the IRS all funds being held for you, to the extent of the levy. (Note: Special rules apply to salary.)

Certain types of property are exempt by law from levy:

1. Apparel and schoolbooks. (Expensive items of apparel such as furs are luxuries and are not exempt from levy.)

2. Fuel, provisions, furniture, and personal effects, not to exceed $1,500 in value (for the head of a household).

3. Books and tools used in your trade, business, or profession, not to exceed $1,000 in value.

4. Unemployment benefits.

5. Undelivered mail.

6. Certain annuity and pension payments (including Social Security benefits).

7. Workers' compensation.

8. Salary, wages, or other income subject to a prior judgment for court-ordered child-support payments.

9. A minimum amount of wages, salary, and other income --$75 per week--plus an additional $25 for each legal dependent.

The IRS is now seizing personal residences more frequently. After a Notice of Seizure is placed on the front door of your house, you have 10 days to come up with the money you owe, or there is an excellent chance that it will be sold at auction to satisfy the tax bill. The house may be redeemed at any time within 180 days after the sale by paying the purchaser the amount paid for the property, plus interest. (By law, the purchaser must sell.)

What Do You Do If You Can't Pay Your Taxes?

Can the IRS put you in jail because you owe it money and have failed to pay, even though the debt has been outstanding for years? The answer is no. Unless you fraudulently conceal your assets or otherwise conspire to beat the government out of its money, no crime has been committed merely because you can't afford to pay your taxes.

The best way to approach the situation of having fallen behind in the payment of taxes is to respond immediately to all

notices sent you requesting payment. Make every attempt to speak to someone at the IRS and follow up the conversation with a confirming letter. Depending upon the facts and circumstances involved, the IRS may be willing to enter into an installment agreement for payment of the outstanding taxes. Usually, such a part payment agreement requires a down payment, followed by monthly payments over a year or 18 months. If you fail to comply with the terms of the part payment agreement, which also requires that all current taxes be paid on time, the agreement becomes void and your property is then subject to levy and seizure.

The best time to try to get the IRS to offer you an installment agreement is at the beginning of the collection process. If you have ignored IRS attempts to work out an arrangement and it is now at your door with a Notice of Seizure, it is extremely unlikely that a part payment agreement will be offered.

What Rights Do You Have in the Collection Division?

Except for statutory rights concerning notice of demand for payment, there are not too many things you actually have a legal right to when it comes to the Collection Division.

For a start, the IRS has no obligation to accept your offer of a part payment agreement. Whether to accept is generally a decision made by the Revenue Officer (and possibly an immediate supervisor). If you feel that the Revenue Officer and supervisor (Group Manager) are being unreasonable, you should immediately attempt to speak to the Branch Chief (the Group Manager's boss) and then to the Chief, Collection Division (the Branch Chief's boss). After exhausting that chain of command, even your Representative in Congress probably can't help--although if you can get your Representative to intervene, the IRS might take a second look at your case.

Bankruptcy is one alternative for staying collection action. It does not discharge your tax liability. If a petition for bankruptcy is filed, the IRS is precluded from selling your property at auction.

How to Negotiate a Settlement When You Owe Money

The first step in negotiating a settlement of taxes owed is to provide the IRS with a current financial statement. Without a statement it can verify, the IRS will not even consider a settlement. What should you do if you don't want the IRS to know about certain assets you own? Just don't furnish the financial statement. It's better to offer no statement at all than offer one that is misleading or fraudulent.

If the IRS already knows about all of your assets, and there is no disadvantage in providing a financial statement, then go ahead and submit the statement. The IRS will be interested in knowing how much money you receive each month, how much is spent, and where. When you complete the personal living expense portion of the form, it is generally a good idea to arrange for some money to be left over each month to pay taxes. The IRS is more inclined to go along with a part payment offer if it feels confident there is money available to make the agreement work.

If you have no assets and no income, there is nothing the IRS can levy. If you are in this desperate predicament, it does provide an opportunity to discuss an Offer in Compromise with the IRS.

An Offer in Compromise is a little-publicized procedure whereby the IRS will accept a one-time payment of as little as 10¢ for each $1 owed in settlement of your tax debt. If the IRS feels it will receive more money from you in the long run by entering into an Offer in Compromise and a collateral agreement (an agree-

ment whereby you agree to pay a certain percentage of your income for 5 to 10 years), it may agree to the compromise.

The best chance of successfully using the Offer in Compromise route is when the tax debt has been on the books for a number of years. The IRS must be convinced that conventional collection procedures won't work. That's why a relatively recent tax obligation will not be settled this way. But if the IRS has had a chance to collect and hasn't succeeded, it is likely to accept your compromise offer.

Here's a tip you should bear in mind: Always use a tax pro to get you through the Offer in Compromise procedure.

Chapter 10
Dealing with Special Agents

Special Agents are IRS employees assigned to the Criminal Investigation Division (CID). Their job is not to put people in jail (a common misconception), but rather to gather the evidence necessary for the IRS to develop a criminal tax case. Once the Special Agent has successfully completed an assignment, the case is referred to the Justice Department for prosecution by the United States Attorney's office.

The primary purpose of the active IRS role in the area of criminal investigations is to promote the voluntary compliance of all taxpayers. If the IRS can gain substantial publicity from the tax-evasion conviction of a prominent local businessperson, the deterrent effect spreads quickly.

The Traps

Contrary to what many people envision, the typical Special Agent presents himself or herself in a low-key, even friendly manner. The goal, after all, is to collect evidence to support the government's contention that a tax crime has been committed. It is sometimes easier to obtain that evidence by playing a "nice guy" role.

If you are the subject of a criminal investigation, it is imperative that experienced counsel be retained to protect your rights and to prepare the best possible defense. The time to involve a lawyer is right at the beginning of an investigation, not when the IRS has already developed its case against you.

One trap that many people who are subjects of criminal investigations fall into is believing that if they answer all of the Special Agent's questions honestly and even volunteer infor-

mation about their misdeeds, the agent will either go easy on them or just go away. Nothing could be further from the truth. All that has been accomplished is that the government's job has been made easier. Remember, the government must prove "beyond a reasonable doubt" that a tax crime has been committed. A self-incriminating statement does not leave the Special Agent with much more to do than wrap up the case and recommend prosecution.

Another trap many unsuspecting individuals fall into during a criminal investigation is to lie when they are being questioned by a Special Agent. Lying is a separate crime! The Special Agent typically will not challenge misleading statements you make at the interview. Rather, these statements will be introduced by the government at your trial to help prove that you intended to break the law and/or that any defense you raise at the trial is not credible because you lied during the investigation.

One problem in dealing with Special Agents is that you may not know that the person you are talking to is a Special Agent. A tactic now used by the Criminal Investigation Division in its effort to develop cases against people suspected of committing tax crimes is the use of undercover operatives. For example, one successful project is called "BOP" for Business Opportunities Project. This undercover operation might involve a Special Agent responding to an advertisement in the business section of the local newspaper soliciting a buyer for a business. Usually two Special Agents will approach the targeted owner for the purpose of negotiating a price for the business. Inevitably, the conversation turns to the fact that cash is skimmed and that there is a second set of books. Now the Special Agents know how much money is not being reported and have all the evidence they need to close the case.

How the IRS Builds a Criminal Case

It may be comforting to know that the Criminal Investigation Division is actually developing fewer cases than it was a number of years ago. However, the number of successful convictions has increased. This means that the IRS is concentrating its efforts on building quality case referrals to the Justice Department.

After a criminal investigation has been authorized, the Special Agent assigned to the case usually does not call the suspect to arrange an appointment or otherwise give advance notice. Rather, the agent shows up at the home or place of business and starts asking questions. The element of surprise is used in the hope of gaining an advantage. The Special Agent hopes that the suspect will make incriminating statements or otherwise provide leads that would not have been provided had the suspect been able to consult with an attorney. Typical questions are:

- Did you report all of your income?
- Where do you keep your savings and checking accounts?
- What kind of car do you own?
- What is the procedure for reporting sales in your business?
- Do you gamble?
- How much cash did you have on hand at the beginning of the year?

The agent is trying to establish not only that a taxpayer failed to report some income but that it was done with the intention of evading tax. If you fail to report a substantial amount of income because you don't know you have earned it, the requisite intent to evade is missing, so there is no crime. Such a situation can arise when a stockbroker sells some of your securities without your knowledge.

In an effort to establish both the amount of income you did not report and to gather evidence to support the position that you intended to evade tax, the Special Agent will subpoena copies of checking account statements, cancelled checks, savings accounts, deposit and withdrawal tickets, signature cards, and application forms for bank loans. The agent may also talk to neighbors and business associates. A search will be made of public records to find out when cars, boats, and real estate were acquired and how much they cost. Insurance policies will be examined to ascertain ownership of furs, jewelry, or antiques. Even passports will be examined in an effort to determine if expensive overseas vacations were reconstructed as business trips or to determine if currency is being transported.

Mail surveillance is another investigatory technique. Agents can determine who your customers and suppliers are and contact them to gain leads to business transactions that may not have been reported. Although the IRS cannot open a taxpayer's mail, it can usually tell all it needs to know by looking at the outside of envelopes. All the IRS must do is request and secure assistance from the local Postal Inspector--no court order is required.

To establish unreported income, the IRS relies most often on bank deposits. It adds up all the taxpayer's bank deposits for the year and subtracts deposits that clearly come from nontaxable sources (loans, gifts, inheritances, and transfers between accounts). The balance is assumed to be income.

Another method that may be used is the net worth analysis. The value of all the taxpayer's property at the beginning of the year is added up. Then the end-of-year assets are totaled. The difference (with adjustments for appreciation, nontaxable income, gifts, inheritances) represents the increase in the taxpayer's net worth for the year. It is assumed that the taxpayer

had enough income to generate that increase in net worth. Sometimes in the initial interview, a taxpayer will be asked how much cash and property he or she had at the beginning of a year. A taxpayer who does not want to appear too prosperous may say a few hundred dollars and no property to speak of. This opens the door for the IRS to claim that everything owned at the end of the year was acquired during the year and should have been reported as income.

Your Rights

The most fundamental right one possesses is the fifth amendment right against self incrimination. If you are (or may be) the target of a criminal investigation, you are not required to answer any questions you believe to be self-incriminating. In other words, if the answers to those questions can be used as evidence against you in court, there is no compulsion to answer. The IRS has an administrative procedure that requires Special Agents to read you the "Miranda" warning prior to being questioned ("...you have a right to an attorney and anything you say may be used against you in a court of law").

Take advantage of this constitutional right by answering no questions until you have had the opportunity to obtain the advice and counsel of an attorney.

There is limited fifth amendment privilege with respect to your ability to keep potentially incriminating business papers from the government. Case law is constantly evolving and appears to be eroding away the individual's right to protect business papers or accountant's workpapers by claiming fifth amendment privilege.

Undercover operations of the IRS were described earlier in this chapter. Some defense attorneys take the position that such activities amount to entrapment. The courts have been reluc-

tant to rule that when a Special Agent poses as someone else, that is entrapment. Note that a Special Agent may not gain evidence by claiming to be a Revenue Agent. However, if the same Special Agent claims to be a butcher and expresses interest in buying a suspect's butcher shop, there is no entrapment.

A final note: Many criminal cases are referred to the Criminal Investigation Division by Revenue Agents who, in the course of an audit, discover unreported income. Be very careful what you or your accountant represents or shows to a Revenue Agent if you know that you did not report all of your income.

Chapter 11
Filing Amended Tax Returns

If you forgot to claim a deduction or credit you were entitled to or there has been a retroactive change in the law, you may want to consider filing an amended tax return. An amended tax return does not automatically subject you to an audit, but it could generate an audit if the return contains an unusual item. More on that later in this chapter.

The Best Time to File
An Amended Tax Return

The best time is one week before the statute of limitations expires. (If the statute of limitations expires on April 15 in any given year, the time to file is April 8.) Thus, if the IRS decides to conduct an audit, the worst it can do is disallow the deductions claimed on the amended return. It cannot get any more tax. If the amended tax return is filed too far in advance of the expiration of the statute of limitations, the IRS will have the opportunity not only to disallow the claim on the amended return but to audit other items on your return for that year. Further, the IRS may decide to audit returns for previous years not yet protected by the statute of limitations.

Safest Amendments

The following changes made to your tax return will probably not result in an audit:

- Amending the return to make use of income averaging to compute the tax.

- Amending the return to make use of the special 10-year averaging method for paying the tax on lump sum pension plan distributions.

• Changing your filing status from married filing separately to joint.

• Taking an energy credit you forgot to claim.

• Taking an investment credit for property you purchased for your business.

Not So Safe Amendments

Filing an amended return to take a deduction for the following may result in an audit because of the high susceptibility of these items to audit:

• Travel and entertainment expenses.

• Unreimbursed business expenses.

• Casualty losses.

• Transactions with relatives.

• Charitable donations of property.

• Home office deductions.

Retroactive Changes in the Law

Certain changes in the tax law give you the right to deductions you couldn't have taken on your original return. Many are in red-flag areas, so be prepared to document and defend your claim if you decide to file for a refund. If the statute of limitations has not yet expired (3 years from the due date of the tax return [April 15] or the date it was actually filed if after April 15), consider these retroactive changes:

Business deductions for club dues were banned by a 1978 law. This law was later repealed, retroactively.

The IRS refused in the past to allow employees any home-office deductions for secondary or sideline businesses. Congress has now eased the rules governing home-office deductions and the new rules apply retroactively.

In the past, if you rented part of your home to a relative, you could deduct expenses only up to the amount of rent collected. No losses were allowed. Here, too, Congress liberalized the law. You may now be able to deduct losses that were previously barred.

Appendix

Document 1: Tax Court Petition

Document 2: Request for Place of Trial

Tax Court Petition

UNITED STATES TAX COURT

(FIRST)	(MIDDLE)	(LAST)
JOHN	B.	SMITH

(PLEASE TYPE OR PRINT)   Petitioner(s)

V.

COMMISSIONER OF INTERNAL REVENUE

Respondent

Docket No. _____

PETITION

1. Petitioner(s) disagree(s) with the tax deficiency(ies) for the year(s) _____1985_____ , as set forth in the NOTICE OF DEFICIENCY dated __July 1, 1986__ , A COPY OF WHICH IS ATTACHED. The notice was issued by the Office of the Internal Revenue Service at _____New York, N.Y._____
(CITY AND STATE)

2. Petitioner(s) taxpayer identification (e.g. social security) number(s) is (are)

111-22-3333

3. Petitioner(s) dispute(s) the following:

Year	Amount of Deficiency Disputed	Addition to Tax (Penalty) if any, Disputed	Amount of Over-payment Claimed
1985	$3,475.00		

4. Set forth those adjustments, i.e. changes, in the NOTICE OF DEFICIENCY with which you disagree and why you disagree.

    1.   The Commissioner erred in disallowing various business expenses

       which are ordinary and necessary costs incurred in the course of

       the taxpayer's occupation.

Petitioner(s) request(s) that this case be conducted under the "small tax case" procedures authorized by Congress to provide the taxpayer(s) with an informal, prompt, and inexpensive hearing at a reasonably convenient location. Consistent with these objectives, a decision in a "small tax case" is final and cannot be appealed to higher Courts (the Courts of Appeals and the Supreme Court) by the Internal Revenue Service or the Petitioner(s). *

7/20/86

SIGNATURE OF PETITIONER	DATE	PRESENT ADDRESS—STREET, CITY, STATE, ZIP CODE—TELEPHONE NO.

SIGNATURE OF PETITIONER (SPOUSE)	DATE	PRESENT ADDRESS—STREET, CITY, STATE, ZIP CODE—TELEPHONE NO.

SIGNATURE AND ADDRESS OF COUNSEL, IF RETAINED BY PETITIONER(S)	DATE

* **If you do not want to make this request, you should place an "X" in the following box.** ☐

T.C. Form 2
(Rev. Feb. 1979)

Request for Place of Trial

UNITED STATES TAX COURT

JOHN B. SMITH)
—————————————————————————)
Petitioner(s),)
)
v.)   Docket No.
)
COMMISSIONER OF INTERNAL REVENUE,)
Respondent.)

REQUEST FOR PLACE OF TRIAL

        Petitioner(s) hereby request(s) that trial of this case be
held at _____New York, N.Y._____.
              (City and State)

                          ————————————————————————————
                          Signature of Petitioner or Counsel

                          Dated: _____July 20_____, 19 86____

                                                  Form 4
                                                  (Rev. 11/76)